D0568135

COOL

FLEXAGON ART

CREATIVE ACTIVITIES THAT MAKE MATH & SCIENCE
FUN FOR KIDS!

A Division of ABDO

ABDO

ANDERS HANSON

AND ELISSA MANN

VISIT US AT WWW.ABDOPUBLISHING.COM

Published by ABDO Publishing Company, a division of ABDO, P.O. Box 398166, Minneapolis,
Minnesota 55439. Copyright ® 2014 by Abdo Consulting Group, Inc. International copyrights
reserved in all countries. No part of this book may be reproduced in any form without written
permission from the publisher. Checkerboard Library™ is a trademark and logo of ABDO Publishing
Company.

Printed in the United States of America, North Mankato, Minnesota
062013
092013

 PRINTED ON RECYCLED PAPER

Design and Production: Anders Hanson, Mighty Media, Inc.
Series Editor: Liz Salzmann
Photo Credits: Anders Hanson, Shutterstock

LIBRARY OF CONGRESS CATALOGING-IN-PUBLICATION DATA

Hanson, Anders, 1980-
Cool flexagon art : creative activities that make math & science fun for kids! / Anders Hanson and
Elissa Mann.
    pages cm. -- (Cool art with math & science)
Includes index.
ISBN 978-1-61783-821-7
1. Polyhedra--Models--Juvenile literature. 2. Geometry, Solid--Models--Juvenile literature.
3. Mathematical recreations--Juvenile literature. 4. Paper work--Juvenile literature. I. Mann, Elissa,
1990- II. Title.
QA491.H355 2013
516'.156--dc23
                        2013001902

CONTENTS

COOL

FLEXAGON ART

HIDDEN IN THE FOLDS

Flexagons are toys made of folded paper. The paper is folded so some parts are hidden. When the folds are **flexed**, they reveal the hidden parts!

Once you've mastered the basic flexagons, there's even cooler stuff to make. Build a transforming paper star. Or try your hand at a 3-D flexagon!

Most flexagons are flat. You can see the front and back. But there are more faces. They can't be seen until the paper is flexed.

3-D flexagons have an extra dimension. You can turn them inside out!

POLYGON BASICS
SIDES, VERTICES, AND ANGLES

Flexagons are made up of shapes called polygons. A polygon is a flat shape with straight sides. Each point where two sides meet is called a vertex. For any polygon, the number of sides equals the number of vertices. For example, a square has four sides and four vertices.

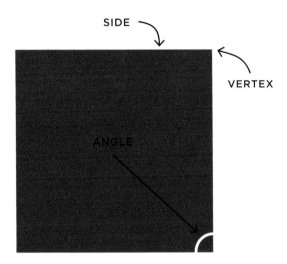

A SQUARE

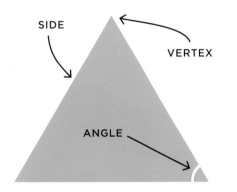

A TRIANGLE

When two lines meet at a vertex, they form an angle. Angles are measured in degrees.

All polygons are either convex or concave. Convex polygons are more common. In a convex polygon, all of the vertices point away from the center of the shape. In a concave polygon, at least one vertex points in toward the center. Both shapes below are hexagons. They each have six sides.

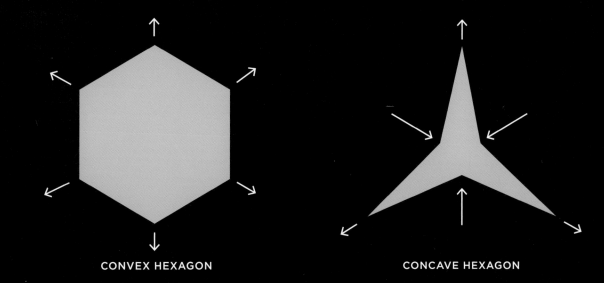

CONVEX HEXAGON

CONCAVE HEXAGON

IN THE FOLD
TYPES OF FLEXAGONS

M ost flexagons have a square or hexagonal shape. Square flexagons are called tetra flexagons. They are made of smaller folded squares. Hexagonal flexagons are called hexa flexagons. They are made of folded triangles.

COMMON FLEXAGON TYPES

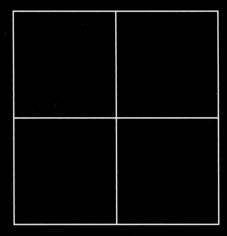

TETRA FLEXAGON

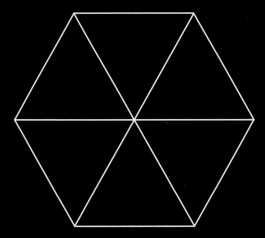

HEXA FLEXAGON

Some flexagons have more hidden faces than others. The total number of faces a flexagon has is indicated by a **prefix** added to its name. For example, a tri-tetra flexagon is a square flexagon with three faces. A tetra-tetra flexagon is a square flexagon with four faces.

TRI-HEXA WHAT?!

Think about the words unicycle, bicycle, and tricycle. Each word has a different prefix. Uni means one, bi means two, and tri means three. They are called number prefixes. A number prefix indicates how much of something there is.

A unicycle has one wheel and a bicycle has two wheels. How many wheels does a tricycle have? How many wheels would a hexa-cycle have?

NUMBER	PREFIX
1	UNI
2	BI
3	TRI
4	TETRA
5	PENTA
6	HEXA
7	HEPTA
8	OCTA
9	ENNEA
10	DECA

FOLDING TIPS
MAKE IT EASIER!

M aking flexagons is fun! It's even more fun when your projects turn out well. Use the tips on these pages to help.

Use **origami** paper or lightweight card stock. If the paper is too thin, the flexagon may tear or wrinkle. If the paper is too thick, it will be difficult to fold and crease.

For glue, use flat-drying paste. It won't warp the paper. Scrapbooking glues, such as Yes! Paste, work well. Don't use too much, though. A little glue goes a long way.

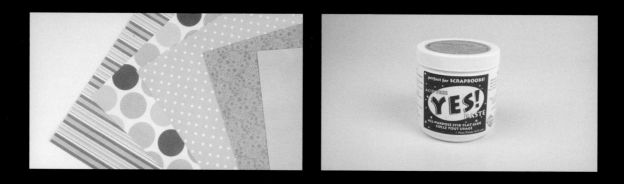

If you struggle with a project, take a break and come back to it later. It's easier to solve problems when you aren't **frustrated**.

If you use a **template**, make the folds exactly on the lines. The more **accurate** the folds, the easier it will be to **flex** it.

After making a fold, run a fingernail firmly along it. That's called creasing. It makes sure the fold is set. Wooden craft sticks work well too.

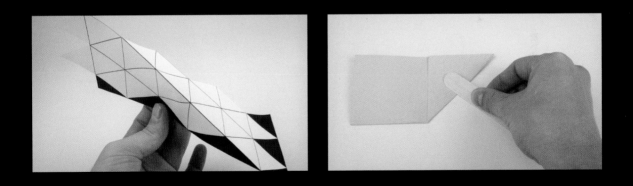

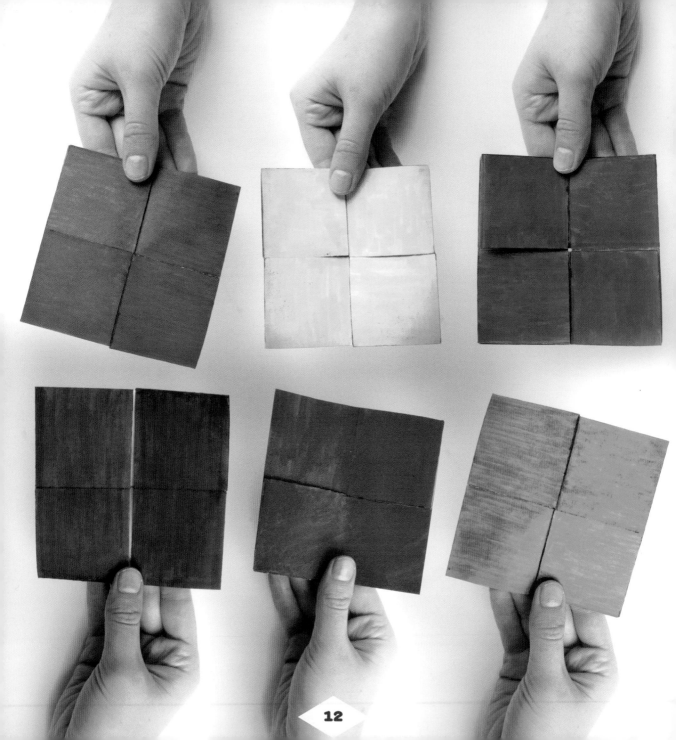

PROJECT

1

MAKE A HEXA-TETRA FLEXAGON

STUFF YOU'LL NEED

- SQUARE PIECE OF PAPER
- PENCIL
- SCISSORS
- MARKERS

TERMS

- ROTATE
- SQUARE
- FACE

A hexa-tetra flexagon is a square flexagon with six faces. Fold it in half and open it like a book. Hidden faces are revealed!

HOW TO MAKE IT

1 Fold the square paper in half. Crease it and then unfold it. Fold it in half the other direction. Crease it and then unfold it.

2 Bring one edge to meet the center crease. Crease it and then unfold it. Rotate the paper a quarter turn to the right.

3 Repeat step 2 three times. The paper should be divided into 16 squares. Draw along the creases with a pencil.

4 Cut out the four middle squares.

5 Label the squares on one side with the letters AABCCBAABCCB. Start in the top left square and go clockwise. Write one letter in each square. Color the squares that have the same letter the same color.

6 Flip the paper over from left to right. Label the squares on one side with the letters DDEFFEDDEFFE. Start at the top left square and go clockwise. Write one letter in each square. Color the squares that have the same letter the same color. Use different colors than you used on the other side.

7   Flip the paper back over from left to right. Fold the left edge to the center.

8   Fold the top edge down to the center.

9   Fold the right edge to the center.

10 Unfold the bottom left fold. Pull the visible D square up. Underneath will be another D square. Pinch the D squares together. Pull the D squares through the center opening of the paper. Twist them under the E square.

11 Fold the top half of the square back. The middle fold should point upward. Open the paper like a book. Rotate the square a quarter turn. Repeat fold. Open. Repeat to find every face of the flexagon.

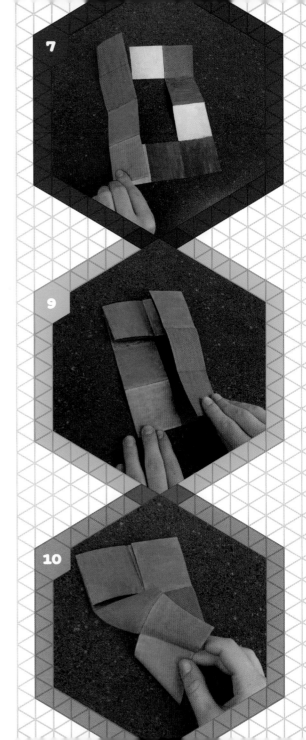

PROJECT

2

MAKE A HEXA-HEXA FLEXAGON

◆◆◆◆◆◆◆

A hexa-hexa flexagon is hexagonal. It has a total of six faces. Four faces are hidden. You can write secret messages or draw maps on them. Only your friends will know how to find your messages!

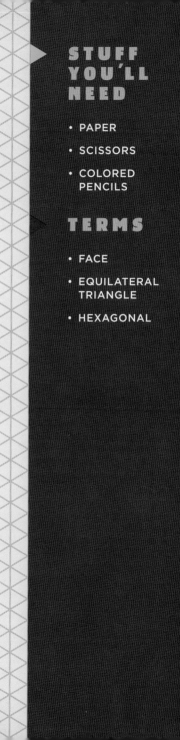

HOW TO MAKE IT

1. Draw a row of 19 equilateral triangles. Cut out the row of triangles. Fold and crease the strip along each line.

2. Lay the strip flat with the long edge on the bottom. Label the triangles with the letters ABCABCABCABCABCABC. Label one letter per triangle. Color the triangles that have the same letter the same color.

3. Flip the strip over. Keep the long edge on the bottom. Label the triangles with the letters DDEEFFDDEEFFDDEEFF. Label one letter per triangle. Color the triangles that have the same letter the same color.

4. Turn the strip back over with the long edge on the bottom. Fold the left two triangles under and down. The B triangle should be behind the C triangle next to it. Then fold the A triangle under and down. It should be behind the B triangle next to it. Keep folding until you get to the end of the strip.

5. Now you should have a shorter, folded strip. Lay it down with an A triangle on the left. A C triangle should be on the right.

6 Fold the left half underneath the right half. You should now see four A triangles.

7 Fold the two triangles on the right down so they are on top. You should now see five A triangles.

8 Fold the bottom two triangles up and underneath. Glue the two blank triangles together.

9 **Flex** your flexagon! Pinch two of the triangles together so that one point of every triangle is pointing up. Fold one of the sides back to reveal a new face. Continue to pinch and unfold to see all the different faces of the flexagon.

3-D GEOMETRY
FROM SHAPES TO SOLIDS

So far you've been working with flat shapes. Now let's look at 3-D solids! A polyhedron is a 3-D **version** of a polygon. A polyhedron has flat faces and straight edges.

Body (3-D) The body is the total space a polyhedron takes up. It is measured in terms of volume.

Faces (2-D) The surface of a polyhedron is made of flat polygons. The edges of the polygons join together. The polygons are called faces. Faces are measured in terms of area.

A point has no dimension. It has no shape that can be measured. A line has one dimension, length. A flat surface has two dimensions, length and width. A 3-D object has three dimensions, length, width, and height. How many dimensions do you have?

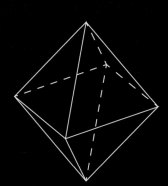

Edges (1-D) The frame, or skeleton, of a polyhedron is made of straight edges. The edges are measured in terms of length.

Vertices (0-D) The edges of a polyhedron meet at points. The points are called vertices. They have no dimension.

PROJECT 3

MAKE A 3-D FLEXAGON

STUFF YOU'LL NEED

- COPIER OR SCANNER
- MARKERS OR COLORED PENCILS
- SCISSORS
- GLUE
- FOAM BRUSH

TERMS

- 3-D
- DIMENSION
- FACE
- ROTATE
- TRIANGLE

Time to add some dimension! This 3-D flexagon has four faces. One of them is hidden from view. The cool thing about this project is how it moves. It unfolds **outward** from its center as it rotates!

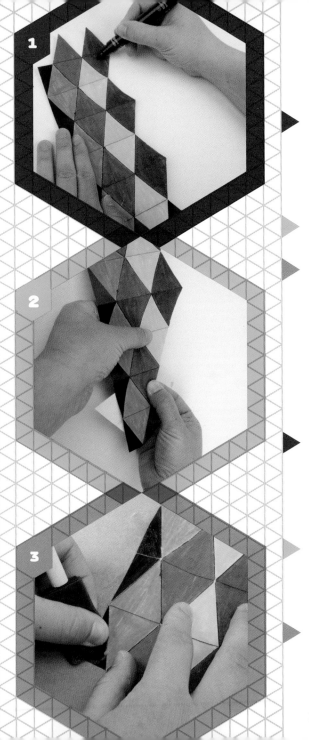

HOW TO MAKE IT

1. Copy the **template** on the opposite page. Cut away the gray parts. Leave the black parts. Color each long row of triangles a different color.

2. Crease the template along all of the lines.

3. Lay the template down with the colored side up. The black triangles should be on the left side. Put glue on on all six black triangles.

(see opposite page for the next three photos)

4. Fold the side with the black triangles back. Line up the colored triangles over the black triangles. Press them so the glue sticks.

5. Bring the ends together. Line the colored triangles up over the black triangles. Press them so the glue sticks. Let the glue dry.

6. To **flex** the flexagon, gently press on the outside edge. A new color will appear.

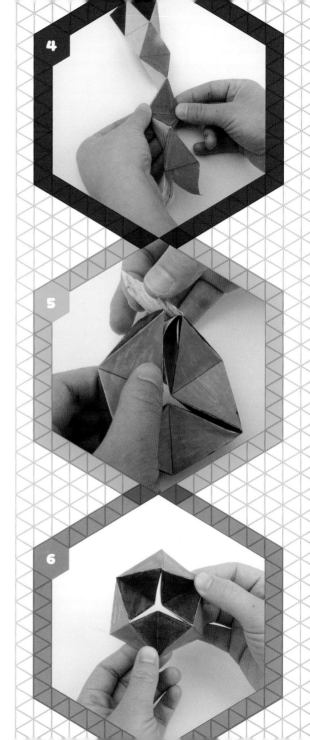

PROJECT

4

TRANSFORMER STAR

◆ ◆ ◆ ◆ ◆ ◆ ◆

This amazing star changes into an octagon! Just push or pull the pieces. Watch it transform. Impress your friends with the star's shape-changing **ability**. Or have fun throwing it like a Frisbee!

STUFF YOU'LL NEED

- 8 SQUARES OF PAPER

TERMS

- OCTAGON
- PARALLELOGRAM
- SQUARE

HOW TO MAKE IT

1 Start with a square sheet of paper. Fold it in half. Crease it. Lay it down with the fold on the left.

2 Fold up the bottom-left corner to meet the right side. Fold and crease.

3 Open the paper up. Bring the two top corners down to the middle of the paper. Fold and crease.

4 With one hand, start to bring the left edge to the right edge. With your other hand, push the center of the bottom edge up. It should be in between the sides as you fold it. Crease the folds.

5 The folded shape is a parallelogram. It has a pocket on one side. It has a point on the other side. Repeat steps 1 through 4 with seven more sheets of paper.

6 Connect the pieces. **Insert** one piece into the pocket of a second piece. Fold the tips of the first piece down. They will be inside the pocket of the second piece.

7 Insert a third piece into the pocket of the second piece. Fold the tips of the second piece inside the pocket of the third piece.

8 Add the fourth, fifth, and sixth pieces the same way. You should have two pieces left.

9 Put the pocket of the seventh piece around the point of the first piece. Put the pocket of the eighth piece around the point of the seventh piece. The eighth piece's point should be in the sixth piece's pocket. Fold all the tips down.

10 Pull and push the sides to change the shape.

3-D - having length, width, and height and taking up space.

DIMENSION - the measurement of extension in one direction. Length, width, and height are all dimensions.

EQUILATERAL TRIANGLE - a triangle with sides that are all the same length.

FACE - a polygon that forms one of the flat surfaces of a 3-D shape.

HEXAGONAL - having six sides and angles.

OCTAGON - a polygon with eight sides and eight angles.

PARALLELOGRAM - a four-sided shape in which the opposite sides are the same length and parallel.

ROTATE - to turn on or around on a center.

SQUARE - a shape with four straight, equal sides and four equal angles.

TRIANGLE - a shape with three straight sides.

GLOSSARY

ABILITY - the skill or power to do something.

ACCURATE - exact or correct.

FLEX - to bend or stretch something.

FRUSTRATED - discouraged or upset because something isn't working or going well.

INSERT - to stick something into something else.

ORIGAMI - the Japanese art of paper folding.

OUTWARD - away from the center.

PREFIX - a letter or group of letters at the beginning of a word that affects the meaning of the word.

TEMPLATE - a shape you draw or cut around to copy it onto something else.

VERSION - a different form or type from the original.

WEB SITES

To learn more about math and science, visit ABDO Publishing Company on the World Wide Web at www.abdopublishing.com. Web sites about creative ways for kids to experience math and science are featured on our Book Links page. These links are routinely monitored and updated to provide the most current information available.

INDEX